CHRISTMAS

A Story by

Eleanor Roosevelt

Illustrated by
FRITZ KREDEL

NEW YORK: ALFRED · A · KNOPF

1 9 4 0

THE TIMES *are so serious that even children should be made to understand that there are vital differences in people's beliefs which lead to differences in behavior.*

This little story, I hope, will appeal enough to children so they will read it and as they grow older, they may understand that the love, and peace and gentleness typified by the Christ Child, leads us to a way of life for which we must all strive.

ELEANOR ROOSEVELT

ST. NICHOLAS'S EVE, 1940, was cold and the snow was falling. On the hearth in Marta's home there was a fire burning, and she had been hugging that fire all day, asking her mother to tell her stories, telling them afterwards to her doll.

3

◇◇◇◇◇◇◇◇◇◇◇◇◇◇◇◇◇◇◇◇◇◇◇◇◇◇◇◇◇◇◇◇

This was not like St. Nicholas's Eve of last year. Then her father had come home. Seven-year-old Marta asked her mother to tell her the story over and over again, so her mother, whose fingers were never idle now that she was alone and had to feed and clothe herself and Marta, sat and knit long woolen stockings and talked of the past which would never come again, and of St. Nicholas's Eve 1939.

The war was going on in Europe in 1939, but Jon was only mobilized. He was just guarding the border, and was allowed to come home for the holiday. Marta's mother said:

"On Monday I got the letter and on

◇◇◇◇◇◇◇◇◇◇◇◇◇◇◇◇◇◇◇◇◇◇◇◇◇◇◇◇◇◇◇◇◇

Tuesday, St. Nicholas's Eve, he came. I got up early in the morning and started cleaning the house. I wanted everything to shine while your father was home. Soon I called you, and when you were dressed and had had your breakfast, you took your place in the window watching for him to come. Every time you saw a speck way down the road, you would call out to me, but I had time to get much of the holiday cooking prepared and the house in good order before you finally cried: 'Here he is,' and a cart stopped by our gate. You threw open the door and ran down the path. I saw him pick you up in his arms, but he was in such a

◇◇◇◇◇◇◇◇◇◇◇◇◇◇◇◇◇◇◇◇◇◇◇◇◇◇◇◇◇◇

hurry that he carried you right on in with him and met me as I was running half-way down the path."

Her mother always sighed and Marta wondered why her eyes looked so bright, then she would go on and tell of Jon's coming into the house and insisting on saying: *"Vroolijk Kerstfeest,"* meaning "Merry Christmas," all over again to her and to Marta, just as though he had not greeted them both outside.

Marta's mother had been busy making cakes, *"bankletters"* and *"speculaas,"* just a few since that year none of the family or friends could come to spend St. Nicholas's Eve with them, for

◇◇◇◇◇◇◇◇◇◇◇◇◇◇◇◇◇◇◇◇◇◇◇◇◇◇◇◇◇◇◇

no one could spend money to travel in such anxious times. She and Marta had saved and saved to get the food for the feast, and now that was in the larder waiting to be cooked.

They both felt sorry that the two grandmothers and the two grandfathers could not come that year, for Jon and big Marta had lived near enough to their parents so that they could often spend the holidays together. Little Marta loved to think about her grandfathers. One grandfather could tell her so much about the animals and the birds and make them seem just like people, and her mother's father could tell her stories, long, long stories, about

◇◇◇◇◇◇◇◇◇◇◇◇◇◇◇◇◇◇◇◇◇◇◇◇◇◇◇◇◇◇◇◇◇◇

things that happened in cities, about processions and having seen the Queen, and so many wonderful things that she could dream about after the visit was over.

Besides, it meant that both her grandmothers helped her mother, and that gave her mother more time to go out with her, so it really was a disappointment when the grandparents could not be with them for this St. Nicholas's Eve. Little Marta did not know it, but to her father's parents it was more than a disappointment. They had wanted so much to see their son again. Like all mothers, his mother feared the worst where her own boy was concerned. Perhaps she had had a premonition of what the future held, but, as with all peasants, the hard facts of life are there to be counted, and the money saved for the trip would keep food in the larder if the winter was going to be as hard as everything indicated, so they did not travel.

Marta's mother had told her that perhaps St. Nicholas, on his white horse with his black servant, Peter, would not bring any presents that year to fill her wooden shoes, but Marta would not believe it. Her first question to her father was: "Will St. Nicholas forget us?"

"No, little Marta," said her father.

"The good Saint, who loves little children, will come tonight if you go to bed like a good girl and go quickly to sleep."

Marta put her little shoes down by the big fireplace, and her mother took her into the bedroom and tucked her away behind the curtains which shielded her bunk along the wall on the cold winter night.

Then there had been a long quiet time when Jon and Marta's mother sat together and talked a little, Jon telling what life was like for the army on the frontier and then lapsing into that complete silence which can only come to two people who are very fond of

◇◇

each other. After a while Jon opened
up his knapsack and took out the
things he had managed to bring to fill
those little wooden shoes, and the
package which held the last present
from her husband that Marta's mother
was ever to receive. With it was the
usual rhyme:

To a busy little housewife
From one who thinks of her
*   through strife,*
To keep her safe from all alarm
And never let her come to harm,
Is all he dreams of night and day
And now forever "Peace" would
*   say.*

◇◇◇◇◇◇◇◇◇◇◇◇◇◇◇◇◇◇◇◇◇◇◇◇◇◇◇◇◇◇◇◇◇◇

Needless to say, she guessed the giver before they went to bed.

On Christmas morning Marta woke and ran to look for her wooden shoes. "St. Nicholas has been here," she cried, "and he's given me many sweets, a doll, and bright red mittens just like the stockings mother made me as a Christmas gift." Then the whole family went skating on the river and there were many other little girls with their fathers and mothers. Everyone glided about and the babies were pushed or dragged in their little sleds. The boys and girls chased one another, sometimes long lines took hands and, after skating away, gathered in a circle, go-

◇◇◇◇◇◇◇◇◇◇◇◇◇◇◇◇◇◇◇◇◇◇◇◇◇◇◇◇◇◇

ing faster and faster until they broke
up because they could not hold on any
longer.

Then at last they went home to dinner. On the table a fat chicken and a
good soup.

At first they ate silently and then as
the edge of their hunger wore off, they
began to talk.

"Marta," said her father, "have you
learned to read in school yet? Can you
count how many days there are in a
month?"

"Oh, yes," replied Marta, "and
Mother makes me mark off every day
that you are gone, and when we are
together we always say: 'I wonder if

Father remembers what we are doing now,' and we try to do just the things we do when you are home so you can really know just where we are and can almost see us all the time."

Her father smiled rather sadly and then her mother said:

"Jon, perhaps it is good for us all that we have to be apart for a while, because we appreciate so much more this chance of being together. There is no time for cross words when you know how few minutes there are left. It should make us all realize what it would be like if we lived with the thought of how quickly life runs away before us. But you are so busy, Jon, you do not have time to think about us much in the army, do you?"

A curious look came into his eyes and Jon thought for a moment with anguish of what he might have to do some day to other homes and other children, or what might happen to his, and then he pulled himself together and you could almost hear him say: "This at least is going to be a happy memory," and turning to Marta, he began to tease her about her fair hair, which stuck out in two little pigtails from the cap which she wore on her head. Seizing one of them he said:

"I can drive you just like an old horse. I will pull this pigtail and you

◇◇◇◇◇◇◇◇◇◇◇◇◇◇◇◇◇◇◇◇◇◇◇◇◇◇◇◇◇◇◇

will turn this way. I will pull the other one and you go that way."

Peals of laughter came from Marta, and before they knew it, the meal was over and the dishes washed and she had demanded that they play a make-believe game with her new doll, where she was a grown-up mother and they had come to see her child.

Such a jolly, happy time, and then as the dusk fell, Marta's father put on his uniform again, kissed her mother, took Marta in his arms, and hugged her tightly, saying: "Take good care of Moeder until I come back."

Then he was gone and they were alone again. The year seemed to travel

heavily. First letters came from Jon, and then one day a telegram, and her mother cried and told Marta that her father would never come back, but her mother never stopped working, for now there was no one to look after them except God and He was far away in His heaven. Marta talked to Him sometimes because mother said He was everyone's Father, but it never seemed quite true. Marta could believe, however, that the Christ Child in the Virgin's arms in the painting in the church was a real child and she often talked to Him.

Strange things Marta told the Christ Child. She confided in Him that she never had liked that uniform which her father went away in. It must have had something to do with his staying away. He had never gone away in the clothes he wore every day and not come back. She liked him best in his everyday clothes, not his Sunday ones, which made him look rather stiff, but his nice comfortable, baggy trousers and blouse. She was never afraid of him then, and he had a nice homey smell; something of the cows and horses came into the house with him, and like a good little country girl Marta liked that smell. She told the Christ Child that her mother had no time to play with her any more. She had to work all

◇◇◇◇◇◇◇◇◇◇◇◇◇◇◇◇◇◇◇◇◇◇◇◇◇◇◇◇◇◇

the time, she looked different, and sometimes tears fell on her work and she could not answer Marta's questions.

There was no school any more for her to go to and on the road she met children who talked a strange language and they made fun of her and said now this country was theirs. It was all very hard to understand and she wondered if the Christ Child really did know what was happening to little children down here on earth. Sometimes there was nothing to eat in the house, and then both she and her mother went hungry to bed and she woke in the morning to find her mother gone and

◇◇◇◇◇◇◇◇◇◇◇◇◇◇◇◇◇◇◇◇◇◇◇◇◇◇◇◇◇◇◇◇◇◇

it would be considerably later before her mother returned with something for breakfast.

Thinking of all these things as her mother told the story again, on this St. Nicholas's Eve, 1940, Marta took off her wooden shoes and put them down beside the open fire. Sadly her mother said: "St. Nicholas will not come tonight," and he did not. Marta had an idea of her own, however, which she thought about until Christmas Eve came. Then she said to her mother: "There is one candle in the cupboard left from last year's feast. May I light it in the house so the light will

◇◇◇◇◇◇◇◇◇◇◇◇◇◇◇◇◇◇◇◇◇◇◇◇◇◇◇◇◇◇◇◇◇◇◇◇◇◇◇

shine out for the Christ Child to see His way? Perhaps He will come to us since St. Nicholas forgot us."

Marta's mother shook her head, but smiled, and Marta took out the candle and carefully placed it in a copper candlestick which had always held a lighted candle on Christmas Eve.

Marta wanted to see how far the light would shine out into the night, so she slipped into her wooden shoes again, put her shawl over her head, opened the door, and slipped out into the night. The wind was blowing around her and she could hardly stand up. She took two or three steps and looked back at the window. She could

see the twinkling flame of the candle, and while she stood watching it, she was conscious of a tall figure in a dark cloak standing beside her.

Just at first she hoped the tall figure might be her father, but he would not have stood there watching her without coming out into the candlelight and picking her up and running into the house to greet her mother. She was not exactly afraid of this stranger, for she was a brave little girl, but she felt a sense of chill creeping through her, for there was something awe-inspiring and rather repellent about this personage who simply stood in the gloom watching her.

◇◇◇◇◇◇◇◇◇◇◇◇◇◇◇◇◇◇◇◇◇◇◇◇◇◇◇◇◇◇◇

Finally he spoke:

"What are you doing here, little girl?"

Very much in awe, Marta responded: "I came out to make sure that the Christ Child's candle would shine out to guide His footsteps to our house."

"You must not believe in any such legend," remonstrated the tall, dark man. "There is no Christ Child. That is a story which is told for the weak. It is ridiculous to believe that a little child could lead the people of the world, a foolish idea claiming strength through love and sacrifice. You must grow up and acknowledge only one superior, he who dominates the rest of the world through fear and strength."

This was not very convincing to Marta. No one could tell her that what she had believed in since babyhood was not true. Why, she talked to the Christ Child herself. But she had been taught to be respectful and to listen to her elders and so silence reigned while she wondered who this man was who said such strange and curious things. Was he a bad man? Did he have something to do with her father's going away and not coming back? Or with her mother's worrying so much and working so hard? What was he doing near her house anyway? What was a bad man like? She had never known one.

He had done her no harm—at least, no bodily harm—and yet down inside her something was hurt. Things could be taken away from people. They had had to give up many of their chickens and cows because the government wanted them. That had been hard because they loved their animals and they had cared for them and it meant also that they would have little to eat and much less money when they lost them, but that was different from the way this man made her feel. He was taking away a hope, a hope that someone

could do more even than her mother
could do, could perhaps make true the
dream, that story she told herself every
night, both awake and asleep, of the
day when her father would come
home, the day when hand in hand they
would walk down the road again together. When he would put her on his
shoulder and they would go skating on
the canal. Somehow this man hurt that
dream and it was worse than not having St. Nicholas come. It seemed to
pull down a curtain over the world.

Marta was beginning to feel very
cold and very much afraid, but all her
life she had been told to be polite to
her elders and ask for permission to do

anything she wished to do. She said:
"I am hoping the Christ Child will
come. May I go in now and will you
not come into my house?"

The man seemed to hesitate a min-
ute, but perhaps he decided it would
be interesting to see the inside of such
a humble home where there was so
much simple faith. In any case, he
wanted to impress upon this child and
upon her mother that foolish legends
were not the right preparation for living in a world where he, the power,
dominated, so he followed Marta into
the house without knocking. Marta's
mother, who had been sitting by the
fire knitting when Marta went out, was

<><><><><><><><><><><><><><><><><><><><><><>

still there, yes, but in her arms was a baby and around the baby a curious light shone and Marta knew that the Christ Child had come. The man in the door did not know, he thought it was an ordinary room with an ordinary baby in a woman's arms.

Striding in, he said: "Madam, you have taught this child a foolish legend. Why is this child burning a candle in the hope that the Christ Child will come?"

The woman answered in a very low voice: "To those of us who suffer, that is a hope we may cherish. Under your power, there is fear, and you have created a strength before which people

⬦⬦⬦⬦⬦⬦⬦⬦⬦⬦⬦⬦⬦⬦⬦⬦⬦⬦⬦⬦⬦⬦⬦⬦⬦⬦

tremble. But on Christmas Eve strange things happen and new powers are sometimes born."

Marta was not interested any more in the tall figure in the cloak. The Christ Child was there in her mother's lap. She could tell Him all her troubles and He would understand why she prayed above everything else for the return of her father. St. Nicholas would never again leave them without the Christmas dinner and she could have the new doll, and the sweets which she longed to taste again. Perhaps if only she went to sleep like a good little girl, there would be a miracle and her father would be there. Off she trotted to the second room, slipped off her shoes, and climbed behind the curtain.

Marta could not go to sleep at once, because though there was no sound from the other room, she still could not free herself from the thought of that menacing figure. She wondered if he was responsible for the tears of the little girl up the road whose father had not come home last year and who had not been visited either by St. Nicholas.

Then before her eyes she suddenly saw a vision of the Christ Child. He was smiling and seemed to say that the little girl up the road had her father this year and that all was well with her.

◇◇◇◇◇◇◇◇◇◇◇◇◇◇◇◇◇◇◇◇◇◇◇◇◇◇◇◇

Marta was happy, fathers are so very
nice. Perhaps if she prayed again to
the Christ Child, when she woke up
He would have her father there too,
and so she said first the prayer she had
always been taught to say and then
just for herself she added: "Dear Christ
Child, I know you will understand that
though God is the father of all of us,
He is very, very far away and the
fathers we have down here are so much
closer. Please bring mine back so that
we can have the cows, the pigs and the
chickens again and all we want to eat
and the tears will not be in my mother's
eyes." The murmur of her prayer died
away as she fell asleep.

A long time the power stood and watched Marta's mother, and finally there came over him a wave of strange feeling. Would anyone ever turn eyes on him as lovingly as this woman's eyes turned on that baby? Bowing low before her, he said: "Madam, I offer you ease and comfort, fine raiment, delicious food. Will you come with me where these things are supplied, but where you cannot keep to your beliefs?"

Marta's mother shook her head and looked down at the baby lying in her lap. She said: "Where you are, there is power and hate and fear among people, one of another. Here there are

◇◇◇◇◇◇◇◇◇◇◇◇◇◇◇◇◇◇◇◇◇◇◇◇◇◇◇◇◇◇◇◇

none of the things which you offer, but there is the Christ Child. The Christ Child taught love. He drove the money-changers out of the temple, to be sure, but that was because He hated the system which they represented. He loved His family, the poor, the sinners, and He tried to bring out in each one the love for Him and for each other which would mean a Christlike spirit in the world. I will stay here with my child, who could trust the legend and therefore brought with her into this house the Christ Child spirit which makes us live forever. You will go out into the night again, the cold night, to die as all must die who are not born

◇◇◇◇◇◇◇◇◇◇◇◇◇◇◇◇◇◇◇◇◇◇◇◇◇◇◇◇◇◇◇◇◇◇

again through Him at Christmas time."

The man turned and went out, and as he opened the door, he seemed to be engulfed in the dark and troubled world without. The snow was falling and the wind was howling, the sky was gloomy overhead. All that he looked upon was fierce and evil. These evil forces of nature were ruling also in men's hearts and they brought sorrow and misery to many human beings. Greed, personal ambition, and fear all were strong in the world fed by constant hate. In the howling of the wind he heard these evil spirits about him, and they seemed to run wild, unleashed with no control.

This has happened, of course, many times in the world before, but must it go on happening forever? Suddenly he turned to look back at the house from which he had come. Still from the window shone the little child's candle and within he could see framed the figure of the mother and the Baby. Perhaps that was a symbol of the one salvation there was in the world, the heart of faith, the one hope of peace. The hope he had taken away from Marta for the moment shone out increasingly into the terrible world even though it was only the little Christ Child's candle.

With a shrug of his shoulders, he turned away to return to the luxury of

◇◇◇◇◇◇◇◇◇◇◇◇◇◇◇◇◇◇◇◇◇◇◇◇◇◇◇◇◇◇

power. He was able to make people suffer. He was able to make people do his will, but his strength was shaken and it always will be. The light in the window must be the dream which holds us all until we ultimately win back to the things for which Jon died and for which Marta and her mother were living.